DECLUTTER YOUR MIND

Finding Clarity in a Busy World

LAUREL Z. HARRETT

Table of Contents

"Decluttering the mind is a journey to rediscover your brilliance beneath the chaos." - Luminita D. Saviuc

Introduction

In today's fast-paced and demanding world, finding clarity and peace of mind can feel like an elusive goal. The constant barrage of information, responsibilities, and distractions can leave us feeling overwhelmed and mentally cluttered. The pressures of work, school, relationships, and societal expectations can consume our thoughts and drain our energy. We may find ourselves constantly juggling multiple tasks, struggling to keep up with the demands of our daily lives.

In this state of mental clutter, our ability to think, make sound decisions, and focus on what truly matters becomes compromised. Our minds are pulled in many different directions, and we lose sight of our priorities and goals. We may feel stuck, stressed, and disconnected from our inner wisdom.

However, amidst this chaotic backdrop, it is important to remember that clarity and peace of mind are not unattainable ideals. Despite the external pressures and the internal chatter, it is possible to navigate through the chaos and find a sense of calm and clarity.

"Declutter Your Mind: Finding Clarity in a Busy World" is a transformative journey that empowers individuals to reclaim their mental clarity. This book is not just about decluttering physical spaces or organizing schedules; it is about decluttering the mind—the core of our being. It is about stripping away the layers of mental noise and distractions to reveal the essence of who we truly are.

By embarking on this journey, you are committing yourself—a commitment to finding inner peace, clarity, and purpose amidst the busyness of everyday life. You are ready to let go of the mental baggage that weighs you down and prevents you from living a fulfilling and joyful life.

Throughout the pages of this book, you will discover practical strategies, powerful insights, and transformative practices to declutter your mind and find lasting clarity. Drawing from the wisdom of mindfulness, simplification, stress management, cognitive restructuring, goal setting, and mindful technology use, this book offers a comprehensive approach to decluttering the mind in every aspect of your life.

But remember, this journey is not a quick fix or a one-size-fits-all solution. It is a process—a deeply personal and transformative process. Each chapter will guide you to explore different aspects of your mind, to question the beliefs and patterns that no longer serve you, and to cultivate new ways of thinking, being, and living.

As you delve into the following chapters, be open to self-reflection, introspection, and growth. Embrace the exercises, practices, and insights shared with an open heart and mind. This is your opportunity to redefine what truly matters to you, align your actions with your values, and create a life that reflects your authentic self.

So, take a deep breath, let go of the external noise for a moment, and embark on this journey of self-discovery and transformation. By the end of this book, you will emerge with a renewed sense of clarity, purpose, and empowerment. You will have the tools and knowledge to navigate the busyness of life with grace and ease, and to find peace within yourself, regardless of the external circumstances.

Are you ready to declutter your mind and embark on this transformative journey? Let's begin.

The Significance of Finding Mental Clarity

A cluttered mind can significantly hinder our ability to function optimally. It leads to decreased focus and concentration, making it difficult to complete tasks efficiently and effectively. When our thoughts are scattered and fragmented, it becomes challenging to stay present and fully engage with the present moment.

Moreover, a cluttered mind often accompanies heightened levels of stress. The constant influx of information, obligations, and responsibilities can overload our mental capacity, leaving us feeling overwhelmed and drained. The resulting stress can negatively impact our physical and emotional well-being, leading to exhaustion, irritability, and even burnout.

Furthermore, a cluttered mind limits our creativity and problem-solving abilities. When our thoughts are clouded and disorganized, it becomes challenging to think outside the box and generate innovative ideas. Clarity of mind, on the other hand, opens up space for creativity to flow freely, allowing us to approach challenges with fresh perspectives and innovative solutions.

By attaining mental clarity, we unlock a range of benefits that positively impact our overall well-being. With a clear mind, we enhance our decision-making abilities, allowing us to make choices that align with our values and goals. Clear thinking empowers us to prioritize effectively, identifying what truly matters and acting accordingly.

Moreover, mental clarity cultivates a sense of calm and inner peace. It helps us develop resilience in the face of challenges, enabling us to navigate life's ups and downs with greater equanimity. As our mental clutter dissipates, we experience heightened self-awareness and a deeper connection to our authentic selves.

In addition, a clear mind enhances our relationships and interactions with others. When mentally cluttered, our attention is divided, and we may struggle to fully engage and connect with the people around us. However, with mental clarity, we can be fully present in our relationships, actively listening and empathizing with others.

Overall, the significance of finding mental clarity cannot be overstated. It is a transformative state of being that enables us to navigate the complexities of a busy world with clarity, purpose, and resilience. By shedding the mental clutter and cultivating clarity, we can optimize our productivity, enhance our well-being, and experience a deep sense of fulfillment and joy.

As we embark on this journey toward mental clarity, we invite readers to recognize the detrimental effects of a cluttered mind and the potential for positive transformation. Embracing the quest for mental clarity is an act of self-care and self-empowerment, laying the foundation for a more fulfilling and balanced life.

Overview of Themes and Key Elements

This section provides an overview of the key themes and elements that form the foundation of this transformative journey toward mental clarity.

Themes:

1. **Mindfulness and Self-Awareness:** The theme of mindfulness and self-awareness emphasizes the importance of being present in the moment and cultivating a deep understanding of one's thoughts, emotions, and inner experiences. It involves practices such as meditation, mindful breathing, and self-reflection to develop a heightened sense of self-awareness and foster a clear and focused mind.

2. **Simplification and Minimalism:** The theme of simplification and minimalism focuses on the process of letting go of physical and mental clutter to create space for clarity and peace of mind. It encourages individuals to simplify their environments, commitments, and thought patterns. By embracing a minimalist lifestyle and reducing distractions, individuals can experience greater mental clarity and a deeper sense of contentment.

3. **Stress Management and Relaxation:** The theme of stress management and relaxation addresses the detrimental effects of stress on mental clarity and overall well-being. It provides techniques and strategies to effectively manage stress, reduce anxiety, and promote relaxation. Through practices such as deep breathing exercises, mindfulness-based stress reduction, and self-care activities, individuals can create a calm and harmonious inner environment.

4. **Cognitive Restructuring and Positive Thinking:** The theme of cognitive restructuring and positive thinking explores the power of our thoughts in shaping our mental clarity. It involves recognizing and challenging negative thought patterns and replacing them with positive and empowering beliefs. By

reframing our perspectives, cultivating self-compassion, and practicing gratitude, individuals can transform their mindsets and enhance their mental well-being.

5. **Prioritization and Goal Setting:** The theme of prioritization and goal setting emphasizes the importance of aligning actions with values and setting meaningful goals. It provides practical tools and techniques to identify priorities, manage time effectively, and achieve a sense of fulfillment. By establishing clear goals and prioritizing tasks, individuals can reduce mental clutter and focus their energy on what truly matters.

6. **Digital Detox and Mindful Technology Use:** The theme of digital detox and mindful technology use recognizes the impact of technology on mental clutter. It encourages individuals to establish healthy boundaries with digital devices, practice digital detox techniques, and engage in mindful technology use. By fostering a balanced relationship with technology, individuals can reduce distractions, enhance focus, and promote mental clarity.

Key Elements:

1. **Real-Life Examples and Stories:** The book incorporates real-life examples and stories to illustrate the transformative power of decluttering the mind. These relatable anecdotes demonstrate how individuals from different backgrounds have successfully navigated their journeys toward mental clarity. By sharing these stories, readers can gain inspiration and insights into their uttering process.

2. **Practical Exercises and Actionable Steps:** Practical exercises and actionable steps are provided throughout the book to help readers apply the concepts and techniques discussed. These exercises offer hands-on experiences that encourage self-reflection, introspection, and personal growth. By actively engaging with the exercises, readers can integrate the teachings into their daily lives and experience tangible results.

3. **Research and Expert Insights:** The book incorporates research findings and expert insights to provide a solid foundation for the strategies and techniques presented. These evidence-based perspectives add depth and credibility to the content, allowing readers to trust the information and understand the underlying principles behind each approach.

4. **Interactive Elements:** To enhance the learning experience, the book includes interactive elements such as reflection questions, journaling prompts, and mindfulness practices. These interactive elements encourage readers to actively engage with the material, fostering self-awareness, and deepening their understanding of the concepts presented.

5. **Visual Aids:** Visual aids play a crucial role in enhancing comprehension and making the content more engaging. The book incorporates visual elements such as diagrams, charts, and illustrations to visually represent concepts and ideas. These visuals help readers grasp complex information more easily and remember key points. Whether it's a visual depiction of the mind's clutter or a diagram illustrating the steps to decluttering, these visual aids provide a visual roadmap for readers to follow and reinforce their understanding of the content.

6. **Testimonials and Success Stories:** Testimonials and success stories are included throughout the book to provide inspiration and motivation. These firsthand accounts from individuals who have successfully decluttered their minds serve as powerful examples of the transformative power of the strategies and techniques presented. By sharing their experiences and the positive outcomes they have achieved, these testimonials instill hope and belief in readers that they too can find clarity and peace of mind.

7. **Encouragement and Empowerment:** Throughout the book, readers are provided with words of encouragement and empowerment. The language used is uplifting and supportive, reminding readers that they could change and transform their

lives. By fostering a positive and encouraging tone, the book instills confidence in readers and motivates them to act toward decluttering their minds and finding clarity.

By incorporating these key elements, the book creates a comprehensive and transformative experience for readers. Real-life examples and stories inspire and provide relatability, practical exercises, and actionable steps allow for immediate application of concepts, research, and expert insights provide credibility, interactive elements engage readers actively, visual aids enhance comprehension, and testimonials and success stories offer inspiration and motivation. With these elements in place, readers are equipped with the tools, knowledge, and support to embark on their journey toward decluttering their minds and finding lasting clarity in a busy world.

Chapter 1: Mindfulness and Self-Awareness

Welcome to the transformative sub-chapter on mindfulness and self-awareness. In this section, we explore the profound impact that these practices can have on decluttering the mind and finding clarity in a busy world. Mindfulness and self-awareness serve as powerful tools for cultivating presence, focusing attention, and gaining a deeper understanding of our thoughts and emotions.

Understanding the concept of mindfulness

We begin by introducing the concept of mindfulness—an ancient practice that has gained significant recognition in recent years. Mindfulness involves intentionally bringing our attention to the present moment without judgment. It is about fully experiencing each moment as it unfolds, rather than being lost in regrets about the past or worries about the future.

At its core, mindfulness encourages us to be fully present and to pay attention to the sensations, thoughts, and emotions arising within us and in our surroundings. By intentionally directing our awareness to the present moment, we can break free from the habitual patterns of ruminating over past events or worrying about the future. Instead, we learn to engage with each moment as it is, cultivating a sense of curiosity and openness.

Mindfulness is not about emptying the mind or trying to suppress thoughts and emotions. Rather, it is about observing our inner experiences with a non-judgmental attitude. We learn to acknowledge and accept the thoughts, feelings, and sensations that arise, without labeling them as good or bad. This non-judgmental awareness allows us to observe our experiences with greater clarity and objectivity, enabling us to respond to them with wisdom and compassion.

In practicing mindfulness, we develop the ability to anchor our attention to the present moment, often using an anchor point such as the breath, bodily sensations, or sounds in our environment. By focusing our attention on these anchors, we create a point of stability amidst the constant flux of thoughts and sensations. This anchor serves as a grounding force, allowing us to cultivate a sense of stability and presence.

Mindfulness is not limited to formal meditation practice; it can be incorporated into every aspect of our daily lives. Through mindfulness, we learn to bring awareness to our daily activities, such as eating, walking, or engaging in conversations. We bring a quality of presence and attentiveness to these ordinary moments, allowing us to savor and appreciate the richness of our experiences.

The benefits of mindfulness extend beyond the present moment. Regular mindfulness practice has been shown to reduce stress, enhance focus and concentration, improve emotional regulation, and foster greater overall well-being. By cultivating mindfulness, we develop a greater sense of self-awareness, enabling us to understand our thoughts, emotions, and behaviors more deeply. This self-awareness empowers us to make conscious choices and respond to life's challenges with greater resilience and clarity.

In the context of finding clarity in a busy world, mindfulness becomes an invaluable tool. It allows us to detach from the constant stream of thoughts and distractions, bringing us back to the present moment and the task at hand. By practicing mindfulness, we cultivate a state of calm amidst the chaos, enabling us to navigate challenges with greater clarity and composure.

Throughout this book, we will explore various mindfulness techniques and practices that readers can incorporate into their daily lives. From formal meditation exercises to informal mindfulness moments, readers will learn practical strategies to develop and deepen their mindfulness practice. Through consistent and dedicated effort, readers can tap into the transformative power of mindfulness and uncover a profound sense of clarity, peace, and well-being during a busy and demanding world.

Cultivating present-moment awareness

By embracing the practice of cultivating present-moment awareness, readers can liberate themselves from the constant stream of thoughts and distractions that clutter their minds. Mindfulness allows them to shift their attention away from external busyness and connect with their inner selves, creating space for clarity, calmness, and deep presence to emerge.

This sub-chapter provides practical techniques for incorporating mindfulness into daily life, empowering readers to integrate these practices into their routines. One such technique is mindful breathing exercises, where readers are encouraged to direct their attention to the sensations of the breath as it flows in and out of their bodies. This simple yet powerful practice serves as a reliable anchor amidst the chaos, helping individuals cultivate present-moment awareness and navigate their experiences with clarity and serenity. Here are some practical techniques to incorporate mindful breathing into your daily routine:

- **Breath Awareness:** Find a comfortable position, either sitting or lying down, and bring your attention to your breath. Notice the sensations of the breath as it flows in and out of your body. Focus your attention on the rise and fall of your abdomen or the sensation of air passing through your nostrils. Whenever your mind wanders, gently guide your attention back to the breath, using it as a focal point for present-moment awareness.

- **Counting Breath:** As you breathe in, silently count "one" in your mind. Then, as you breathe out, count "two." Continue counting each breath cycle up to a count of ten, and then start again from one. This technique helps to anchor your attention to the breath and promotes focus and relaxation.

- **Box Breathing:** Visualize a square shape and assign a count to each side of the square. Inhale for a count of four as you trace the first side of the square. Hold your breath for a count of four as you trace the second side. Exhale for a count of four as you trace the third side. Finally, hold your breath again for a count of four as you trace the fourth side. Repeat this pattern, maintaining a slow and steady pace, allowing the breath and the visualization to guide your focus and promote a sense of calm.

- **Mindful Walking:** While walking, bring your attention to the physical sensations of each step. Notice the contact between your feet and the ground, the movement of your legs, and the rhythm of your breath. Engage all your senses in the experience—observe the sights, sounds, and smells around you. If your mind starts to wander, gently guide your focus back to the sensations of walking and breathing.

Incorporating Mindfulness into Daily Life

- **Mindful Eating:** Take the time to savor each bite of food, paying attention to the taste, texture, and aroma. Notice the sensations in your body as you eat. Slow down and bring your full awareness to the present moment during meals, allowing yourself to fully engage with the experience.

- **Mindful Pause:** Throughout the day, take mindful pauses to check in with yourself. Close your eyes, take a few deep breaths, and bring your attention to the present moment. Notice any physical sensations, thoughts, or emotions that arise. This practice can help you recenter, regain focus, and cultivate clarity amidst daily activities.
- **Mindful Listening:** When engaged in conversations, meetings, or even listening to music, practice mindful listening. Give your full attention to the speaker or the sounds, without judgment or anticipation. Be present and receptive, allowing yourself to truly hear and connect with the words or melodies.

- **Mindful Transitions:** Use moments of transition throughout the day—such as when you wake up, before starting a new task, or before going to bed—as opportunities for mindfulness. Take a few mindful breaths, set an intention for the upcoming activity, or reflect on the experiences of the day. These brief moments of mindfulness can help you transition with greater clarity and presence.

Mindful eating is another practice explored in this sub-chapter, emphasizing the importance of savoring, and fully experiencing each bite of food. By bringing mindful awareness to the process of eating, readers develop a deeper appreciation for the flavors, textures, and nourishment that food provides. This practice helps break free from automatic or mindless eating habits, fostering a healthier and more mindful relationship with food.

By incorporating these practical techniques into your daily life, you can cultivate mindfulness and bring a sense of clarity and serenity to your experiences. Remember, mindfulness is not about achieving a particular state of mind but rather about being fully present and accepting of the present moment, including the sensations of the breath as it flows in and out of your body.

The sub-chapter also introduces body scan exercises, which invite readers to develop body awareness—a fundamental aspect of mindfulness. Through systematically directing attention to different parts of the body, individuals become attuned to physical sensations, tension, and relaxation. This practice facilitates a deeper mind-body connection, allowing readers to release tension and cultivate a heightened sense of bodily presence. Here are some practical techniques for incorporating body scan exercises into your routine:

- **Find a comfortable position:** Start by finding a comfortable position, either sitting or lying down, where you can relax and maintain a sense of alertness. Close your eyes if that feels comfortable for you.

- **Begin with the breath:** Bring your attention to the sensations of the breath as it flows in and out of your body. Notice the rise and fall of your abdomen or the sensation of air passing through your nostrils. Allow the breath to serve as an anchor, grounding your awareness in the present moment.

- **Systematically scan the body:** Starting from the top of your head, slowly move your attention down through different parts of your body. Notice any sensations, tensions, or areas of relaxation as you bring your attention to each body part. You can go through the body systematically, from head to toe, or choose to focus on specific areas that need attention or relaxation.

- **Observe sensations with curiosity:** As you scan each body part, maintain a sense of curiosity and non-judgment. Notice any physical sensations, such as warmth, tingling, or pressure. Be aware of any areas of tension or discomfort without trying to change them. Simply observe and acknowledge the sensations as they arise.

- **Release tension and relax:** If you encounter areas of tension or discomfort, bring your attention to those areas and intentionally soften and relax the muscles. Breathe into those areas, imagining that your breath can soothe and release any tension or tightness.

- **Stay present and non-judgmental:** Throughout the body scan, be present with whatever sensations arise. If your mind starts to wander or judgments arise, gently guide your attention back to the body and the sensations you are observing. Practice acceptance and non-judgment, allowing yourself to be fully present with your bodily experience.

- **Complete the body scan:** Continue scanning each part of your body until you reach your toes or any other areas you have chosen to focus on. Take a few moments to sense your body, noticing any shifts or changes in your overall bodily experience.

- **Transition back to the breath:** After completing the body scan, gently bring your attention back to the sensations of the breath. Notice the rhythm and flow of your breath and allow it to anchor you in the present moment.

By regularly practicing body scan exercises, you can develop a deeper sense of body awareness and cultivate a stronger mind-body connection. This practice can help release physical and mental tension, enhance relaxation, and foster a greater sense of presence and well-being in your daily life. Remember to direct your attention to the sensations of the breath as it flows in and out of your body, using it as a focal point for grounding and centering your awareness.

Additionally, the sub-chapter highlights the significance of self-awareness as a complementary practice to mindfulness. Self-awareness involves turning inward and developing a deeper understanding of our thoughts, emotions, and behaviors. It allows individuals to recognize patterns, triggers, and limiting beliefs that contribute to mental clutter.

Here are some key reasons why self-awareness is crucial:

- **Recognizing Patterns:** Self-awareness enables us to identify recurring patterns in our thoughts, emotions, and behaviors. By observing ourselves with curiosity and non-judgment, we can become aware of habits, reactions, and responses that contribute to mental clutter. This recognition empowers us to break free from unhelpful patterns and make conscious choices that promote clarity and well-being.

- **Identifying Triggers:** Through self-awareness, we become attuned to the triggers that activate certain thoughts, emotions, or behaviors. We gain insight into the specific situations, people, or circumstances that tend to disrupt our mental clarity. By recognizing these triggers, we can proactively manage them, create healthy boundaries, and respond with greater clarity and serenity.

- **Uncovering Limiting Beliefs:** Self-awareness allows us to explore our underlying beliefs and assumptions that shape our perception of ourselves and the world. We can uncover self-limiting beliefs that contribute to mental clutter, such as self-doubt or negative self-talk. By identifying these limiting beliefs, we can challenge and reframe them, opening new possibilities and cultivating a more empowering mindset.

- **Cultivating Emotional Intelligence:** Self-awareness facilitates the development of emotional intelligence by helping us understand and navigate our emotions. By observing and acknowledging our emotional experiences without judgment, we gain insight into how certain emotions contribute to mental clutter or hinder our clarity. This awareness allows us to respond to our emotions in a skillful and balanced way, promoting mental clarity and well-being.

- **Taking Responsibility for Growth:** Self-awareness encourages us to take responsibility for our growth and well-being. When we are aware of our thoughts, emotions, and behaviors, we can make conscious choices to change unhelpful patterns, develop healthier coping mechanisms, and foster mental clarity. Self-awareness empowers us to actively participate in our ney of decluttering the mind and cultivating a greater sense of clarity and purpose.

To cultivate self-awareness, reflective exercises, and self-inquiry prompts are provided. Through practices such as journaling or engaging in introspection, readers gain insights into their thought processes, emotional reactions, and habitual behaviors. Self-awareness empowers individuals to recognize when their minds become cluttered and consciously choose how to respond to situations, fostering greater clarity and intentionality in their actions.

As readers engage with the techniques and concepts presented in this sub-chapter, they begin to witness the transformative power of mindfulness and self-awareness in their own lives. They discover their capacity to respond rather than react to challenging situations, to be fully present in their interactions, and to find moments of peace and clarity even amidst the busyness of life.

The sub-chapter concludes by reminding readers that mindfulness and self-awareness are not fleeting practices but ongoing journeys of self-discovery and growth. It encourages them to embrace these practices as a way of life, nurturing their presence and self-awareness daily. Through the cultivation of present-moment awareness, readers can declutter their minds, access a deeper sense of clarity, and embark on a transformative journey toward finding profound clarity in a busy world.

Developing self-awareness and understanding of thoughts and emotions

In this section, we will delve into the fascinating realm of "Developing Self-Awareness and Understanding of Thoughts and Emotions." This practice is a transformative journey that allows you to turn inward and gain a deeper understanding of your thoughts and emotions, leading to enhanced mental clarity and personal growth.

The Power of Self-Awareness

Self-awareness is the foundation of a more meaningful and fulfilling life. By cultivating self-awareness, you gain valuable insights into your thoughts, emotions, and behaviors. This heightened awareness empowers you to recognize patterns and triggers that contribute to mental clutter, enabling you to navigate life with greater clarity and intention.

Embracing the Present Moment

At the heart of self-awareness lies the practice of mindfulness. Mindfulness is the art of being fully present in the here and now. Through mindful breathing exercises and meditation techniques, you can anchor yourself amidst the hustle and bustle of daily life. By paying attention to your breath and focusing on the present moment, you can cultivate a sense of calm and centeredness, helping you to declutter your mind from distractions.

Acknowledging and Understanding Emotions

Understanding and acknowledging your emotions is a crucial aspect of self-awareness. We will guide you on how to embrace your emotions with compassion and without judgment. By allowing yourself to feel and express your emotions, you prevent them from becoming bottled up and overwhelming your mind. This process enables you to find healthier ways to process and navigate your emotional experiences.

Recognizing Thought Patterns

Self-awareness involves recognizing the thought patterns that shape your perceptions and experiences. We will explore various techniques to help you observe your thoughts non-judgmentally. By becoming aware of your thought patterns, you can gain greater control over your mental landscape and break free from self-limiting beliefs. This process allows you to replace negative thought patterns with more positive and constructive ones.

The Journey of Self-Discovery

Developing self-awareness is an enriching journey of self-discovery and continuous learning. As you practice mindful breathing and meditation techniques, you will gradually deepen your understanding of yourself. This journey will open doors to new perspectives and insights, fostering personal growth and empowering you to align your actions with your true self.

Embracing Self-Compassion

Throughout this chapter, we emphasize the importance of self-compassion in the process of self-awareness. Be kind and gentle with yourself as you explore your inner world. Self-compassion nurtures resilience, allowing you to approach self-discovery with patience and understanding. Remember that this journey is about learning and growth, and it is okay to be imperfect along the way.

Unlocking Clarity Within

By delving into the realm of self-awareness and understanding your thoughts and emotions, you will unlock the power of clarity within yourself. Understanding your inner world empowers you to declutter your mind and align your actions with authenticity and purpose. This newfound clarity will serve as a reliable anchor amidst life's challenges, helping you navigate your experiences with serenity and a deeper sense of well-being.

Practicing mindful breathing and meditation techniques

Welcome to the practice of mindful breathing and meditation techniques. In this section, we will explore how these powerful practices can enhance self-awareness, promote mental clarity, and bring a sense of calm and presence to your daily life.

The Art of Mindful Breathing

Mindful breathing is a fundamental technique that forms the cornerstone of mindfulness. It involves bringing your full attention to the present moment by focusing on your breath. Here's how you can practice mindful breathing:

1. Find a quiet and comfortable space where you won't be disturbed.
2. Sit or lie down in a relaxed position, with your spine straight and your hands resting comfortably.
3. Close your eyes and take a few deep breaths to settle into the practice.
4. Begin to pay attention to your breath as it flows in and out of your body. Notice the sensation of the air entering your nostrils, filling your lungs, and leaving your body.
5. If your mind wanders, gently bring your focus back to your breath without judgment.

Guided Meditation for Self-Awareness

Guided meditation is an excellent way to deepen your self-awareness and understanding of your thoughts and emotions. Here's a simple guided meditation to get you started:

1. Find a quiet and comfortable space to sit or lie down.
2. Close your eyes and take a few deep breaths to relax your body and mind.
3. Imagine a peaceful place in nature, such as a serene beach or a lush forest. Visualize yourself in this tranquil setting.
4. Start to observe your thoughts and emotions without getting caught up in them. Imagine them as passing clouds in the sky, coming, and going without attachment.
5. If negative thoughts or emotions arise, acknowledge them with kindness and let them gently drift away like leaves on a stream.
6. Bring your focus back to your breath whenever your mind starts to wander.
7. Stay in this meditative state for a few minutes, allowing yourself to be fully present in the moment.

Benefits of Mindful Breathing and Meditation

Practicing mindful breathing and meditation offers a myriad of benefits, including:

- **Reduced Stress:** By focusing on your breath and being present, you can calm your nervous system and reduce stress levels.

- **Enhanced Self-Awareness:** Mindfulness allows you to become more aware of your thoughts, emotions, and bodily sensations, leading to a deeper understanding of yourself.

- **Improved Concentration:** Regular practice can sharpen your focus and attention, helping you stay present and engaged in your daily activities.

- **Increased Resilience:** Mindfulness fosters resilience, enabling you to respond to life's challenges with greater clarity and equanimity.

- **Better Emotional Regulation:** Mindful breathing and meditation can help you regulate your emotions and cultivate a sense of emotional balance.

As you embark on this journey of self-awareness through mindful breathing and meditation, remember that it is a practice, not a destination. Be patient with yourself and approach it with an open heart and mind. Over time, you will experience the transformative power of these techniques, and they will become valuable tools in your quest for mental clarity and well-being.

With every breath, may you find a deeper connection with yourself and the world around you.

Chapter 2: Simplification and Minimalism: Creating Space for Clarity

Welcome to Chapter 2: Simplification and Minimalism: Creating Space for Clarity. In this chapter, we delve into the profound significance of simplification and minimalism in decluttering the mind and creating a space for clarity to emerge.

Recognizing the Impact of Physical and Mental Clutter

Simplification and minimalism play a profound role in decluttering the mind and creating a space for clarity to emerge. The connection between physical and mental clutter is undeniable. Our external environment often mirrors our internal state, and a cluttered and disorganized physical space can lead to mental chaos and overwhelm. When we are surrounded by a mess, it can be challenging to find focus and peace within ourselves.

By recognizing this impact, you are encouraged to understand that simplifying your physical surroundings is not just about having an orderly home or workspace; it is about creating a harmonious and conducive environment for mental clarity. When we clear out the excess physical possessions that no longer serve a purpose or bring us joy, we create more physical and mental space for the things that truly matter. This process of letting go can be liberating and helps us detach from material possessions, allowing our minds to be freer and at ease.

Beyond physical clutter, simplification and minimalism extend to the realm of commitments and mental baggage. In our fast-paced lives, we often find ourselves entangled in numerous commitments, obligations, and thoughts, leading to overwhelming and a lack of mental clarity. By simplifying our commitments and setting boundaries, we can create more time and space for ourselves to engage in activities that align with our values and bring us joy.

Simplifying mental clutter involves releasing excessive thoughts, worries, and negative self-talk. Our minds can be crowded with constant mental chatter, leaving us mentally exhausted and unable to think clearly. By practicing mindfulness and other relaxation techniques, we can quiet the noise in our minds and cultivate a more focused and calmer mindset. Simplification allows us to let go of mental baggage, making room for clarity, creativity, and positive thinking to thrive.

Embracing simplicity and minimalism in various aspects of life has numerous benefits. It brings a sense of lightness and freedom, allowing us to focus on what truly matters. By reducing stress, overwhelm, and distractions, we can channel our energy toward the things that align with our goals and values. This intentional living brings a greater sense of purpose and contentment, fostering inner peace and well-being.

In summary, simplification and minimalism are powerful tools for decluttering the mind and creating space for clarity to emerge. By recognizing the impact of physical and mental clutter on our well-being, you (the reader) are encouraged to simplify your surroundings, commitments, and thoughts. This intentional and mindful approach to life allows us to let go of what no longer serves us, fostering mental clarity, and creating a space that nurtures inner peace and focus amidst the busyness of the world.

Letting Go of Excess Possessions and Commitments

Here are the practical tips for simplifying possessions:

- **The 3-Rule:** For each item you come across, ask yourself three questions: Do I use it regularly? Do I love it? Does it align with my values and goals? If the answer is "no" to any of these questions, consider letting go of the item.

- **Decluttering Zones:** Divide your living space into different zones (e.g., kitchen, bedroom, study) and tackle one zone at a time. This makes the decluttering process more manageable and less overwhelming.

- **The Marie Kondo Method:** Follow the principles of Marie Kondo, where you hold each item in your hand and ask, "Does it spark joy?" If it doesn't bring you joy, it may be time to let it go.

- **One-In, One-Out Rule:** Implement this rule when buying new items. For every new item you bring into your home, let go of one similar item to maintain balance.

- **Sentimental Items:** For sentimental items, consider taking photos of them to preserve the memories without the physical clutter.

- **Seasonal Decluttering:** Regularly declutter and reevaluate your possessions with each change of season. Donate or sell items you no longer need or use.

Practical Strategies for Simplifying Commitments:

- **Prioritization List:** Create a list of your current commitments and rank them based on importance and alignment with your values. Consider which ones bring you the most joy and fulfillment.

- **Saying "No":** Practice saying "no" to new commitments that do not align with your priorities. Learn to decline gracefully and without guilt.

- **Reviewing Commitments:** Regularly review your existing commitments and assess if they still serve your goals and values. If not, consider reducing or letting go of some.

- **Set Boundaries:** Establish clear boundaries with work, family, and social commitments to avoid overextending yourself. Learn to say "yes" to commitments that truly matter to you.

- **Time Blocking:** Allocate specific time blocks for each commitment and avoid multitasking. This helps you stay focused and prevents feeling overwhelmed.

- **Learn to Delegate:** If possible, delegate certain tasks or responsibilities to others to free up time and energy for activities that matter most to you.

By incorporating these practical tips and strategies into their lives, readers can begin the process of simplifying their possessions and commitments. Letting go of excess belongings and unnecessary obligations creates space for a peaceful and organized living environment, leading to greater mental clarity, calmness, and focus on what truly matters in life. This intentional approach to decluttering allows individuals to create a sense of harmony between their physical spaces and their inner selves, leading to a more fulfilling and purposeful life.

Creating a Minimalist Environment for a Clear Mind

A minimalist environment plays a significant role in fostering a clear mind and promoting mental well-being. By consciously designing spaces that are free from unnecessary clutter and distractions, individuals create an environment that supports clarity, focus, and tranquility. The minimalist approach encourages a deliberate choice of items and aesthetics, allowing for a sense of harmony and calm in our surroundings.

Benefits of Simplicity in Various Aspects of Life

- **Home Environments:** A minimalist home provides a sanctuary from the chaotic outside world. When our living spaces are organized and clutter-free, we experience a sense of peace and relaxation, allowing our minds to unwind and recharge. A clutter-free home also reduces visual distractions, making it easier to focus on tasks and engage in meaningful activities.

- **Workspaces:** A minimalist workspace enhances productivity and creativity. With fewer distractions and a clean, organized desk, individuals can concentrate on their work with greater clarity and efficiency. A clutter-free workspace also contributes to reduced stress and improved mental clarity.

- **Daily Routines:** By simplifying daily routines and eliminating unnecessary complexities, individuals can navigate their days with ease and mindfulness. Simplifying routines helps to reduce decision fatigue and allows us to focus on what truly matters, freeing up mental space for more meaningful pursuits.

The Impact on Mental State

A minimalist environment positively influences our mental state, contributing to a clearer and more focused mind. With fewer distractions, we can concentrate on the tasks at hand without feeling overwhelmed by an abundance of stimuli. This simplicity promotes a greater sense of calm and serenity, reducing stress and promoting a positive mental outlook.

Encouraging Mindful Choices

Simplicity encourages us to be more mindful of our choices, both in the physical items we bring into our lives and in the way we structure our daily activities. By intentionally choosing what we surround ourselves with and how we spend our time, we align our lives with what truly matters to us. This mindful approach leads to a deeper sense of purpose and fulfillment, contributing to mental clarity and a more meaningful existence.

In summary, creating a minimalist environment is instrumental in fostering a clear mind and promoting mental well-being. By embracing simplicity in various aspects of life, including home environments, workspaces, and daily routines, individuals can experience the benefits of reduced stress, improved focus, and a deeper connection with what brings them joy and fulfillment. Intentionally designing spaces that are free from unnecessary clutter and distractions allows individuals to think more clearly and make mindful choices, leading to a life of greater clarity, purpose, and inner peace.

Embracing Simplicity and Its Benefits in Various Aspects of Life

The simplicity extends far beyond decluttering physical possessions and environments. It is a mindset that can be applied to every facet of life, including relationships, habits, and daily choices. Embracing simplicity allows individuals to approach life with a discerning eye, evaluating what truly adds value and meaning.

Benefits of Simplicity in Different Areas of Life

- **Relationships:** Simplifying relationships involves fostering deeper connections with fewer people. By focusing on quality over quantity, individuals can invest their time and energy in nurturing meaningful relationships. This approach leads to more fulfilling and supportive connections, reducing emotional clutter and promoting a sense of belonging.

- **Habits:** Simplifying habits involves streamlining routines and eliminating unnecessary complexities. By establishing simple and consistent habits, individuals can reduce decision fatigue and create more mental space for other important aspects of life. Simplified habits contribute to increased efficiency and overall well-being.

- **Daily Choices**: Embracing simplicity in daily choices involves being mindful of how time and resources are utilized. By making intentional decisions and prioritizing what truly matters, individuals can avoid the trap of overcommitting and feeling overwhelmed. Simplified choices lead to increased focus and a greater sense of control over one's life.

The Benefits of Simplicity:

- **Improved Focus:** Simplifying various aspects of life frees up mental space and reduces distractions, allowing individuals to concentrate on what is truly important. With improved focus, one can engage more deeply in tasks, relationships, and personal growth.

- **Reduced Stress:** A minimalist mindset helps individuals let go of non-essential responsibilities and possessions, reducing the burden of overwhelm and stress. By focusing on the essentials, individuals experience a greater sense of peace and contentment.

- **Increased Productivity:** Simplification allows for greater efficiency and time management. By eliminating unnecessary complexities, individuals can optimize their productivity and accomplish more with less effort.

- **Enhanced Well-being:** Embracing simplicity fosters a deeper appreciation for the present moment and what truly brings joy and fulfillment. By eliminating excess and focusing on what matters, individuals experience a heightened sense of well-being and inner peace.

Simplification with Self-Compassion and Patience

It is important to remember that simplicity is not about depriving oneself or adhering to rigid rules. Rather, it is a journey of intentional choices and mindful consumption. Everyone's path to simplicity is unique, and it is essential to approach it with self-compassion and patience. Simplification is a gradual and ongoing process, and every small step towards a more simplified life contributes to greater mental clarity and contentment.

In conclusion, embracing simplicity in various aspects of life brings a range of benefits, including improved focus, reduced stress, increased productivity, and enhanced overall well-being. By adopting a minimalist mindset and evaluating life with a discerning eye, individuals can create space for clarity, peace, and a greater sense of well-being. It is essential to approach simplification with self-compassion and patience, understanding that the journey towards a more simplified life is personal and unique to everyone. With intentional choices and mindful consumption, individuals can experience the transformative power of simplicity, leading to a life of greater clarity and contentment.

Chapter 3: Stress Management and Relaxation

Identifying Sources of Stress and Their Effects on Mental Clarity

In the fast-paced and demanding world we live in, stress has become a common companion in our daily lives. It is essential to explore the significance of stress management and relaxation as tools to nurture clarity amidst the chaos. By recognizing the sources of stress and understanding its effects on mental clarity, readers can take proactive steps toward enhancing their well-being.

Sources of Stress in Our Lives

Identifying the sources of stress is the first step towards managing its impact on mental clarity. Sources of stress can vary from individual to individual but may include work-related pressures, relationship challenges, financial concerns, health issues, and external demands. Readers are encouraged to reflect on their own lives and pinpoint the specific stressors that may be contributing to mental clutter and overwhelm.

Detrimental Effects of Stress on Mental Clarity

Stress can have a profound impact on mental clarity and cognitive function. It may lead to racing thoughts, difficulty concentrating, memory lapses, and emotional overwhelm. The constant presence of stress can clutter the mind, hindering one's ability to think clearly and make sound decisions. Recognizing the detrimental effects of stress on mental clarity motivates readers to act and prioritize stress management in their lives.

Tools for Stress Management and Relaxation

To cultivate a sanctuary of inner calm amidst the chaos, readers need effective tools for stress management and relaxation. By incorporating these tools into their daily lives, individuals can reduce the impact of stress and improve mental clarity:

- **Breathing Exercises:** Mindful breathing exercises can serve as a reliable anchor amidst the chaos, helping individuals cultivate present-moment awareness and navigate their experiences with clarity and serenity.

- **Body Scan Exercises:** Body scan exercises facilitate a deeper mind-body connection, allowing readers to release tension and cultivate a heightened sense of bodily presence.

- **Self-Awareness Practice:** Turning inward and developing self-awareness helps individuals recognize patterns, triggers, and limiting beliefs that contribute to mental clutter. By understanding themselves better, individuals can proactively address sources of stress and find clarity in their responses to challenging situations.

- **Mindful Technology Use:** Being mindful of technology use allows individuals to reduce digital distractions, promoting mental clarity and presence in daily activities.

- **Relaxation Techniques:** Engaging in relaxation practices such as mindfulness-based stress reduction and self-care activities fosters a sense of calm and tranquility, counteracting the negative effects of stress on mental clarity.

Conclusion

In conclusion, stress management and relaxation are vital tools for nurturing clarity in a busy world. By identifying sources of stress and understanding its impact on mental clarity, readers can take proactive steps towards enhancing their well-being. The integration of mindful practices, relaxation techniques, and self-awareness empowers individuals to navigate life's challenges with greater clarity, focus, and serenity. By cultivating a sanctuary of inner calm amidst the chaos, individuals can declutter their minds and foster a deeper sense of well-being and mental clarity.

Stress Reduction Techniques: Breathing Exercises and Progressive Muscle Relaxation

Breathing exercises are powerful tools for inducing relaxation and promoting mental clarity. Here are some practical techniques that you can incorporate into your daily lives:

- **Diaphragmatic Breathing:** Also known as deep belly breathing, this technique involves placing one hand on the chest and the other on the abdomen. Inhale deeply through the nose, allowing the abdomen to expand and rise while keeping the chest relatively still. Exhale slowly through the mouth, feeling the abdomen fall. This technique calms the nervous system and helps individuals feel more centered and grounded.

- **Box Breathing:** This technique follows a pattern of inhaling, holding the breath, exhaling, and holding the breath again, all for equal counts. For example, inhale for a count of four, hold for four, exhale for four, and hold for four. Repeat this cycle several times. Box breathing helps regulate the breath and promotes a sense of calm and balance.

- **4-7-8 Breathing:** Inhale quietly through the nose for a count of four, hold the breath for a count of seven, and exhale audibly through the mouth for a count of eight. This technique is particularly effective for reducing anxiety and promoting relaxation.

Progressive Muscle Relaxation (PMR):

Progressive muscle relaxation is a technique that helps release physical tension and promote relaxation. Here's how readers can practice PMR:

- o **Find a Comfortable Position:** Sit or lie down in a comfortable position with eyes closed.

- o **Focus on Muscle Groups:** Starting from the feet and working upward, tense and then relax each muscle group for about 5-10 seconds. For example, tense the toes, then release. Move on to the feet, calves, thighs, and so on, until you reach the muscles of the face and scalp.

- o **Notice Sensations:** As you tense and relax each muscle group, pay attention to the sensations in your body. Notice the difference between tension and relaxation.

- o **Breathe Mindfully:** Throughout the exercise, maintain a focus on the breath. Breathe deeply and rhythmically as you release tension from each muscle group.

o **Practice Regularly:** Regular practice of PMR can help individuals become more aware of physical tension and learn to let go of stress in the body.

Conclusion

Breathing exercises and progressive muscle relaxation are effective techniques for stress reduction and promoting mental clarity. By incorporating these practices into their daily routines, readers can activate the body's relaxation response, release tension, and cultivate a sense of calm and inner peace. Whether it's taking a few moments for deep breathing throughout the day or setting aside dedicated time for progressive muscle relaxation, these techniques serve as valuable tools for managing stress, enhancing well-being, and fostering mental clarity amidst the challenges of daily life.

Incorporating Relaxation Practices: Mindfulness-Based Stress Reduction and Self-Care Activities

Mindfulness-based stress reduction is a powerful approach to managing stress and cultivating mental clarity. It involves developing a non-judgmental awareness of one's thoughts, emotions, and bodily sensations in the present moment. Here's how you can incorporate mindfulness into your life:

- **Mindful Breathing:** As mentioned earlier, focus on the breath as it flows in and out of the body. Pay attention to the sensations of the breath, the rise and fall of the abdomen, and the feeling of air passing through the nostrils. When the mind wanders, gently bring the attention back to the breath.

- **Body Scan:** Practice a body scan exercise to develop body awareness. Start from the toes and gradually move attention up through the body, noticing any tension or discomfort and allowing it to release as you breathe. This practice fosters a deeper mind-body connection and helps release physical tension.

- **Mindful Daily Activities:** Bring mindfulness to daily activities such as eating, walking, or washing dishes. Focus on the sensations, tastes, and textures of the experience. By being fully present in each moment, readers can reduce mental clutter and cultivate a sense of calm and centeredness.

Self-Care Activities

Self-care is essential for stress management and relaxation. By nurturing their well-being, readers can replenish their energy and promote mental clarity. Here are some self-care activities to consider:

- **Mindful Movement:** Engage in mindful movement practices such as yoga, tai chi, or qigong. These practices not only promote physical well-being but also help calm the mind and reduce stress.
- **Nature Connection:** Spend time in nature, whether it's taking a walk in the park, sitting by a river, or spending time in the garden. Nature has a calming effect on the mind and helps foster a sense of peace and clarity.

- **Meditation and Guided Imagery:** Practice meditation or listen to guided imagery sessions to relax the mind and reduce stress. These practices can be done at any time and are effective in promoting mental clarity and emotional well-being.

- **Creative Expression:** Engage in creative pursuits such as writing, drawing, painting, or playing a musical instrument. These activities provide a sense of joy and fulfillment and can serve as a form of emotional release.

Conclusion

Mindfulness-based stress reduction and self-care activities are powerful practices for managing stress, decluttering the mind, and fostering mental clarity. By cultivating mindfulness, readers can develop present-moment awareness and respond to stressors with resilience and calmness. Engaging in self-care activities nurtures their well-being, replenishes their energy, and promotes a greater sense of balance and peace.

Incorporating these practices into their daily lives empowers readers to navigate the challenges of a busy world with clarity, focus, and equanimity, ultimately leading to a more fulfilling and harmonious life.

Building Resilience and Coping Strategies to Navigate Stressful Situations

Building resilience and effective coping strategies are essential for navigating the challenges and stressors of life. These skills empower individuals to handle difficult situations with greater ease and maintain a sense of inner calm. Here's why they are significant:

- **Navigating Ups and Downs:** Life is filled with ups and downs, and resilience equips individuals to bounce back from setbacks and adversities. Coping strategies provide the tools needed to manage stress and emotional challenges effectively.

- **Enhancing Mental Well-being:** Resilience and coping skills contribute to improved mental well-being. By developing these skills, individuals can reduce anxiety, manage negative emotions, and cultivate a positive mindset.

- **Embracing Adaptability:** Resilience involves adaptability and the ability to navigate change and uncertainty. In a rapidly changing world, adaptability is a valuable skill that allows individuals to stay grounded and flexible in the face of challenges.

- **Promoting Self-Compassion:** Coping strategies that include self-compassion help individuals treat themselves with kindness and understanding. This self-compassion prevents self-criticism from adding to mental clutter and fosters a healthier relationship with oneself.

Chapter 4: Cognitive Restructuring and Positive Thinking

Understanding the Power of Thoughts and Their Impact on Mental Clarity

Our thoughts are incredibly powerful and shape our perceptions, emotions, and behaviors. They act as the lens through which we view the world and influence how we interpret and respond to situations. Positive thoughts can uplift us, boost our confidence, and enhance mental clarity, while negative thoughts can lead to self-doubt, anxiety, and mental clutter.

The Transformative Power of Reshaping Thoughts

Our thoughts have a profound impact on our emotions, behaviors, and overall well-being. Cognitive restructuring is a powerful technique that allows us to take control of our thoughts, challenge negative patterns, and cultivate a more positive and empowering mindset. By understanding the process of cognitive restructuring, you can unlock the transformative potential of reshaping your thoughts for enhanced mental clarity and emotional well-being.

1. Recognizing Negative Thought Patterns:

The first step in cognitive restructuring is becoming aware of our thought patterns. Negative thoughts often operate on autopilot, influencing how we interpret events and how we feel about ourselves and others. By practicing mindfulness and paying attention to our inner dialogue, we can identify negative thought patterns like self-criticism, catastrophizing, and overgeneralization.

2. Questioning the Validity of Negative Thoughts

Once we recognize negative thought patterns, it is essential to question their accuracy and validity. Often, our negative thoughts are not based on objective reality but are distorted perceptions influenced by past experiences or emotional states. By asking ourselves critical questions like, "Is this thought based on evidence?" or "Are there alternative explanations for this situation?", we can challenge the validity of negative thoughts and begin to loosen their grip on our minds.

3. Reframing Negative Thoughts

After questioning the validity of negative thoughts, we can actively reframe them into more realistic and constructive alternatives. For example, if we catch ourselves thinking, "I always mess up everything," we can reframe it as, "Everyone makes mistakes, and I can learn from this experience to improve next time." This process of cognitive restructuring allows us to create a more balanced and accurate perspective on ourselves and the world around us.

4. Practicing Positive Affirmations

Positive affirmations are another powerful tool in reshaping our thoughts. By repeating positive and empowering statements about ourselves, we reinforce self-belief and counteract the effects of negative self-talk. Examples of positive affirmations include "I am capable and resilient," "I am worthy of love and respect," and "I embrace challenges as opportunities for growth."

5. Embracing Self-Compassion

Cultivating self-compassion is an integral part of reshaping our thoughts. It involves treating ourselves with kindness and understanding, especially during difficult times or when we make mistakes. Instead of harshly criticizing ourselves for perceived failures, self-compassion encourages us to offer ourselves the same care and support we would offer to a friend facing similar challenges.

6. Consistent Practice and Patience

Reshaping our thoughts through cognitive restructuring requires consistent practice and patience. It is essential to recognize that changing thought patterns is not an overnight process and may take time. It is normal to experience setbacks, but with persistence and self-compassion, we can gradually replace negative thought patterns with more positive and empowering ones.

Conclusion

The transformative power of reshaping thoughts lies in our ability to consciously challenge negative patterns and cultivate a positive and empowering mindset. By recognizing negative thought patterns, questioning their validity, reframing them with positive affirmations, and embracing self-compassion, we can enhance our mental clarity and emotional well-being. With consistent practice and patience, cognitive restructuring becomes a valuable tool for decluttering our minds, reducing stress, and approaching life with greater resilience and clarity.

Identifying and Challenging Negative Thought Patterns

Our thoughts play a significant role in shaping our experiences and perceptions. Negative thought patterns can lead to mental clutter, causing us to feel overwhelmed, anxious, and stuck. By identifying and challenging these negative thought patterns, you can gain greater clarity and foster a more positive mindset.

Embarking on a Journey of Self-Discovery

Welcome to the transformative journey of self-discovery! This process will take you on an introspective exploration of your thought patterns and beliefs, inviting you to become more mindful of your inner dialogue and emotional responses to various situations. By engaging in self-reflection and introspection, you will gain valuable insights into yourself and the factors that contribute to mental clutter.

- **Creating Space for Self-Reflection:** Find a quiet and comfortable space where you can reflect without distractions. Carve out time in your day to sit with your thoughts and emotions, allowing yourself to be fully present in the moment.

- **Mindful Awareness of Thoughts:** As you go about your day, pay attention to your thoughts without judgment. Notice any recurring patterns of negative thinking or self-criticism. Be curious about the underlying beliefs that influence these thoughts.

- **Journaling Your Thoughts and Emotions:** Keep a journal to record your thoughts and emotions as you navigate different experiences. Journaling provides an opportunity to express yourself honestly and helps you identify thought patterns that contribute to mental clutter.

- **Recognizing Triggers and Responses:** Be mindful of situations or events that trigger negative thoughts or emotional reactions. Notice how these triggers impact your mental clarity and emotional well-being.

- **Exploring Underlying Beliefs:** When you encounter negative thoughts or emotions, explore the beliefs that underlie them. Ask yourself if these beliefs are based on reality or if they are distorted by past experiences or fears.

- **Questioning Negative Thoughts:** Challenge negative thoughts by asking yourself if they are helpful or if they contribute to mental clutter. Replace them with more realistic and positive alternatives.
- Practicing Mindful Breathing: In moments of stress or overwhelm, practice mindful breathing to anchor yourself in the present. Focus on the sensations of your breath as it flows in and out of your body, allowing it to calm your mind and bring clarity.

- **Cultivating Self-Compassion:** Be kind and understanding towards yourself as you navigate this journey. Remember that self-discovery is a process, and it's okay to encounter challenges along the way. Treat yourself with the same compassion and support you would offer to a friend.

- **Seeking Support:** If you find that certain thought patterns or emotions are particularly challenging to navigate, consider seeking support from a therapist, counselor, or trusted friend. Talking about your experiences can offer new perspectives and insights.

- **Embracing Growth and Change:** Approach this journey with an open mind and a willingness to embrace growth and change. As you become more aware of your thought patterns, you have the power to reshape them and cultivate a more positive mindset.

Remember, self-discovery is a personal and ongoing process. Embrace each step of the journey with curiosity and self-compassion. By exploring your thought patterns and beliefs, you pave the way for greater mental clarity, a deeper understanding of yourself, and the empowerment to declutter your mind from negative thought patterns.

Practical Exercises and Techniques for Cognitive Restructuring

Congratulations on embarking on the journey of cognitive restructuring! As you explore your thought patterns and work towards cultivating a positive mindset, these practical exercises and techniques will serve as valuable tools to support your cognitive restructuring journey.

- **The ABC Technique:** This exercise helps you identify the Activating event, the Beliefs triggered by the event, and the Consequences (emotional and behavioral) of those beliefs. Once you've recognized the consequences, you can challenge and replace negative beliefs with more rational and constructive ones.

- **Thought Record Sheet:** Use a thought record sheet to document your negative thoughts, the situation that triggered them, and the evidence for and against each thought. This process allows you to evaluate the accuracy of your thoughts and encourages a more balanced perspective.

- **Cognitive Reframing:** Practice cognitive reframing by deliberately challenging negative thoughts and finding alternative, more positive ways to view a situation. For example, if you catch yourself thinking, "I'm not good enough for this job," reframe it to "I have valuable skills and experience that make me a strong candidate for this job."

- **Positive Affirmations:** Create a list of positive affirmations that resonate with you. Repeat these affirmations regularly, especially during challenging times, to reinforce positive beliefs about yourself and your abilities.

- **Gratitude Journaling:** Start a gratitude journal to focus on the positive aspects of your life. Each day, write down three things you are grateful for. This practice helps shift your mindset towards positivity and fosters a greater sense of appreciation.

- **Visualization:** Use visualization to imagine yourself successfully navigating challenging situations with a positive mindset. Picture yourself overcoming obstacles and achieving your goals. Visualization can boost your confidence and motivation.

- **Practice Mindfulness Meditation:** Incorporate mindfulness meditation into your daily routine. Mindfulness helps you observe your thoughts without judgment, promoting greater awareness and detachment from negative thought patterns.

- **Engage in Positive Activities:** Participate in activities that bring you joy and fulfillment. Engaging in positive experiences helps counteract the impact of negative thoughts and contributes to a more positive mindset.

- **Challenge Cognitive Distortions:** Identify cognitive distortions, such as black-and-white thinking, overgeneralization, or personalization, and challenge them. Replace distorted thoughts with more balanced and realistic perspectives.
- **Limit Negative Media Exposure:** Be mindful of the media you consume, and limit exposure to negative news or content that can contribute to negative thought patterns. Instead, seek out sources of inspiration and positivity.

Remember that cognitive restructuring is a process that requires patience and consistency. These exercises and techniques are meant to be practiced regularly, gradually reshaping your thought patterns, and cultivating a more positive and empowering mindset. Embrace the journey, be gentle with yourself, and celebrate each small step forward. With dedication and effort, you have the power to declutter your mind from negative thought patterns and create a mental space filled with clarity and optimism.

Reframing Negative Experiences and Fostering a Positive Mindset

Cultivating Self-Compassion

One of the most powerful ways to reframe negative experiences and foster a positive mindset is by cultivating self-compassion. Often, when faced with challenges or setbacks, our inner dialogue can become harsh and critical, leading to feelings of inadequacy and self-doubt. However, practicing self-compassion allows us to treat ourselves with kindness, understanding, and acceptance, just as we would a close friend.

Techniques for Practicing Self-Compassion:

- **Self-kindness:** Whenever you encounter difficulties or make mistakes, be gentle with yourself. Avoid self-criticism and offer yourself words of encouragement and understanding.

- **Recognize Common Humanity:** Remember that everyone faces challenges and experiences ups and downs in life. Recognizing our shared human experience can help us feel less isolated in our struggles.

- **Mindfulness:** Practice mindfulness by becoming aware of your thoughts and emotions without judgment. Observe negative thoughts and emotions without getting caught up in them.

- **Affirmations:** Use positive affirmations to counteract self-critical thoughts. Repeat statements like "I am capable," "I am worthy," and "I deserve compassion."

- **Self-Care:** Prioritize self-care activities that nurture your well-being. Engage in activities that bring you joy and relaxation, such as spending time in nature, reading, or practicing hobbies.

- **Celebrate Achievements:** Acknowledge your accomplishments, no matter how small. Celebrating your successes boosts self-confidence and reinforces a positive mindset.

The Power of Positive Thinking

Positive thinking is a transformative practice that can declutter the mind and create space for a more optimistic and empowering mindset. By focusing on the positive aspects of life, we can rewire our brains to see opportunities and possibilities, even in challenging situations.

Techniques for Positive Thinking:

- **Positive Affirmations:** Use positive affirmations to affirm your strengths, capabilities, and positive qualities. Repeat them regularly to reinforce a positive self-image.

- **Gratitude Exercises:** Practice gratitude by keeping a gratitude journal or taking a few minutes each day to reflect on the things you are thankful for. Cultivating gratitude shifts your focus from what you lack to what you have, fostering a positive outlook.

- **Optimistic Reframing:** When faced with challenges, reframe them as opportunities for growth and learning. Instead of dwelling on what went wrong, focus on the lessons and potential for personal development.

- **Surround Yourself with Positivity:** Surround yourself with positive influences, whether it's supportive friends, uplifting books, or inspiring media. Positive environments nourish a positive mindset.
- **Visualize Success:** Use visualization techniques to imagine yourself succeeding in your endeavors. Visualizing success boosts confidence and motivation.

By practicing self-compassion and embracing positive thinking, readers can break free from the cycle of negativity, cultivate self-acceptance and resilience, and create a mental environment that fosters clarity and inner strength. These practices empower individuals to approach challenges with optimism and navigate life with a sense of purpose and clarity.

Cultivating Self-Compassion and Gratitude to Enhance Mental Well-being

This is the enlightening journey of "Cultivating Self-Compassion and Gratitude to Enhance Mental Well-being." We delve into the transformative power of cognitive restructuring and positive thinking, and how they can profoundly impact our mental clarity and overall well-being.

I want to emphasize that cognitive restructuring and positive thinking are not about denying or suppressing negative emotions. Rather, they offer a powerful way to reframe our thoughts and choose empowering perspectives. By recognizing the power of our thoughts and intentionally shifting them towards positivity, we can declutter our minds from self-limiting beliefs and embrace a more constructive and optimistic outlook on life.

As you engage with the practical exercises and techniques provided in this chapter, you will begin to witness the transformative power of cognitive restructuring and positive thinking in your own life. Through self-discovery and introspection, you will gain a deeper understanding of your thought patterns and beliefs. You will learn to challenge negative self-talk, reframe past experiences, and embrace a mindset that empowers you to navigate the challenges of a busy world with clarity and resilience.

I want to remind you that cognitive restructuring and positive thinking are ongoing practices that require dedication and self-awareness. It's essential to be patient and compassionate with yourself as you embark on this transformative journey. With perseverance and consistency, you can integrate these practices into your daily life, decluttering your mind from negative thought patterns, cultivating self-compassion, and fostering a more optimistic and empowering mindset.

As you continue to embrace these practices, you will find that they have the power to create a profound shift in your mental well-being. By choosing to focus on gratitude and positive affirmations, you can develop a more resilient and joyful approach to life.

I encourage you to wholeheartedly engage with the concepts presented here. Embrace the power of self-compassion and gratitude and witness the positive changes they bring to your life. This chapter is a stepping stone towards a more fulfilled and mentally clear existence.

Chapter 5: Prioritization and Goal Setting

Welcome to the empowering chapter on "Prioritization and Goal Setting: Aligning Actions with Clarity and Purpose." In this chapter, we will explore the significance of prioritization, time management, and goal-setting techniques as powerful tools to help you achieve a sense of fulfillment, accomplishment, and clarity in your life.

Defining Personal Values and Aligning Them with Goals

In this section, we will explore the importance of defining your values and aligning them with your goals. Understanding your core values is crucial for making meaningful decisions and creating a life that aligns with your true self.

Defining Your Values

Personal values are the principles and beliefs that guide your actions and define what matters most to you in life. They serve as a compass, helping you navigate through the complexities of the world and make choices that are in line with your authentic self.

Take some time for self-reflection and introspection. Consider what truly brings you joy, fulfillment, and a sense of purpose. Identify the qualities you admire in others and the moments in life when you felt most alive and content. These reflections will help you uncover your core values, whether they revolve around family, personal growth, community, creativity, or other aspects of life.

Aligning Values with Goals

Once you have a clear understanding of your values, the next step is to align them with your goals. Your goals should reflect what truly matters to you and should contribute to your sense of purpose and fulfillment.

Start by setting SMART (Specific, Measurable, Achievable, Relevant, Time-bound) goals that align with your values. For example, if one of your core values is personal growth, a goal could be to take a course or attend a workshop on a subject that interests you. If family is a core value, a goal could be to spend quality time with your loved ones regularly.

By aligning your goals with your values, you create a deeper sense of meaning and motivation. You will find that pursuing these goals brings you a greater sense of satisfaction and fulfillment because they are in harmony with your authentic self.

Embracing Flexibility and Evolution

It's essential to recognize that personal values and goals are not set in stone. As you grow and evolve, your values and aspirations may change too. Embrace this natural evolution and be open to reassessing your goals periodically. Allow yourself the freedom to adapt and refine your path as needed.

Conclusion

Defining your values and aligning them with your goals is a powerful process that brings clarity and purpose to your life. By staying true to what matters most to you, you can make decisions with confidence and create a life that reflects your authentic self. As you embark on this journey of self-discovery, remember to be kind and patient with yourself, and allow your values to guide you towards a more fulfilling and purposeful existence.

Setting SMART (Specific, Measurable, Achievable, Relevant, Time-bound) Goals

Here we will delve into the concept of setting SMART goals as a powerful technique to achieve clarity and success in your endeavors. SMART goals are Specific, Measurable, Achievable, Relevant, and Time-bound, providing a clear framework for goal setting that increases the likelihood of accomplishing your aspirations.

- **Specific Goals:** A specific goal is well-defined and clear. Instead of setting a vague goal like "improve my health," make it more specific by saying "exercise for 30 minutes five times a week" or "consume five servings of fruits and vegetables daily." The more specific your goal, the easier it is to focus your efforts and measure progress.

- **Measurable Goals:** Measuring your progress is crucial for staying on track and maintaining motivation. Ensure your goals are measurable, so you can assess your achievements objectively. For instance, if your goal is to read more books, set a measurable target like "read 20 pages per day" or "complete one book per month."

- **Achievable Goals:** Your goals should be challenging but attainable. Consider your resources, skills, and time available. Setting overly ambitious goals that are beyond your current capabilities may lead to frustration. Choose goals that stretch you but are within reach with effort and commitment.

- **Relevant Goals:** Make sure your goals align with your values and long-term objectives. Goals that are relevant to your life's purpose will fuel your motivation and sense of fulfillment. Ask yourself if the goal is truly meaningful to you and if achieving it contributes to your overall vision of success.

- **Time-bound Goals:** Set a specific timeframe for accomplishing your goals. Having a deadline creates a sense of urgency and prevents procrastination. For example, if you aim to start a new business, set a time-bound goal like "launch my online store within six months" or "achieve my first sale by the end of the year."
- **Putting SMART Goals into Practice:** Start by identifying the areas of your life where you want to make progress or achieve

something meaningful. Then, break down your aspirations into specific, measurable, achievable, relevant, and time-bound goals. Write them down and review them regularly to track your progress and make any necessary adjustments.

Conclusion

Setting SMART goals is a powerful strategy for aligning your actions with clarity and purpose. By making your goals specific, measurable, achievable, relevant, and time-bound, you increase your chances of success and fulfillment. Remember to approach the goal-setting process with intention and self-compassion, celebrating your achievements and learning from any setbacks along the way.

Effective Time Management Techniques for Prioritization

In this fast-paced world, the ability to align your actions with your true priorities is a skill that can lead to unparalleled clarity, productivity, and fulfillment.

Discovering Your True North

Amid the chaos of daily life, it's easy to lose sight of what truly matters. Through our carefully crafted practical steps and exercises, you will embark on a journey of self-discovery. By engaging in introspection and reflecting on your values, interests, and aspirations, you'll gain profound insights into what holds genuine significance for you. These exercises, which include journaling, introspection, and self-assessment, are your compass to unveiling your priorities.

Navigating the Sea of Time

Time is our most precious resource, and managing it wisely is a cornerstone of leading a purpose-driven life. Our techniques will empower you to deconstruct your daily routines, analyze your commitments, and uncover time sinks that may be hindering your progress. By gaining awareness of your time allocation, you'll be empowered to make mindful choices that are aligned with your goals.

Crafting Goals with Purpose

Setting goals is the bridge between aspirations and achievements. We introduce you to the SMART (Specific, Measurable, Achievable, Relevant, Time-bound) goal-setting framework. With our guidance, you'll learn to articulate goals that are not only actionable but also deeply resonant with your aspirations. Through SMART goals, you'll be charting a course toward manifesting your dreams.

Overcoming Challenges and Sustaining Momentum

The journey of pursuing your goals is not without its challenges. This chapter equips you with strategies to overcome obstacles and maintain unwavering momentum. You'll acquire tools for managing setbacks, fostering resilience, and nurturing a growth-oriented mindset. Armed with these skills, you'll approach hurdles with tenacity and continue progressing toward your objectives.

In Conclusion

As you delve into the realm of effective time management and prioritization, remember that this journey is a testament to your commitment to living a purposeful life. By discovering your authentic priorities, navigating time mindfully, setting meaningful goals, and fostering resilience, you're forging a path toward unparalleled clarity, productivity, and accomplishment.

Overcoming Obstacles and Staying Motivated on the Path to Achieving Goals

In this section, we will explore the importance of overcoming obstacles and staying motivated on your path to achieving your goals. Pursuing your dreams and aspirations can be a challenging journey, but with the right mindset and strategies, you can navigate through obstacles and maintain your motivation.

- **Embrace Resilience:** Obstacles are a natural part of any journey toward success. Embrace the concept of resilience, which is the ability to bounce back from setbacks and adversity. When faced with challenges, view them as opportunities for growth and learning. Remember that setbacks do not define your worth or potential, but rather provide valuable lessons that can propel you forward.

- **Stay Flexible and Adapt:** Life is unpredictable, and circumstances may change. Stay open to adjusting your plans and strategies as needed. Being flexible allows you to respond to unexpected challenges and opportunities that may arise. Embrace change and view it as a chance to explore new possibilities.

- **Break Down Goals into Smaller Steps:** Large goals can feel overwhelming, leading to a loss of motivation. Break down your goals into smaller, manageable steps. Celebrate your progress with each milestone achieved, which will help maintain your momentum and enthusiasm.

- **Visualize Success:** Visualize yourself accomplishing your goals and experiencing the joy and satisfaction that comes with it. Visualization can help reinforce your belief in your abilities and keep you focused on the result.

- **Seek Support and Accountability:** Share your goals with supportive friends, family, or mentors. Having a support system can provide encouragement, motivation, and valuable feedback. Additionally, consider finding an accountability partner who will help keep you on track and motivated.

- **Celebrate Achievements:** Celebrate both small and significant achievements along your journey. Recognize your hard work and progress, as it will boost your confidence and motivation to continue moving forward.

- **Practice Self-Compassion:** Be kind to yourself during challenging times. Avoid self-criticism and negative self-talk. Instead, practice self-compassion by acknowledging your efforts and treating yourself with understanding and kindness. Remember that setbacks are a natural part of the process, and learning from them will make you stronger.

- **Stay Focused on Your "Why":** Reconnect with the reasons why you set your goals in the first place. Understanding your deeper motivations will give you a sense of purpose and determination to persevere even when faced with obstacles.

Conclusion

Overcoming obstacles and staying motivated on the path to achieving your goals is a fundamental aspect of personal growth and success. Embrace resilience, adaptability, and self-compassion as you navigate through challenges. Remember to break down your goals, seek support, visualize success, and celebrate your achievements along the way. With determination and a positive mindset, you can overcome any obstacle and stay motivated to achieve your dreams.

Chapter 6: Digital Detox and Mindful Technology Use

In this chapter, we will explore the impact of technology overload on our mental clarity and well-being. In today's fast-paced digital age, technology has become an integral part of our lives. While it brings numerous benefits and conveniences, excessive technology use can also lead to mental clutter and overwhelm.

Recognizing the Effects of Technology Overload on Mental Clarity

Technology overload refers to the excessive and unbalanced use of digital devices, such as smartphones, computers, and social media platforms. The constant stream of information, notifications, and distractions can lead to reduced focus, increased stress, and diminished mental clarity.

Effects on Mental Clarity

Excessive technology use can contribute to a cluttered mind. The constant exposure to screens and information overload can lead to mental fatigue and difficulty concentrating. It can also disrupt sleep patterns and negatively impact overall well-being.

Finding Balance in the Digital Age

Recognizing the effects of technology overload is the first step toward finding balance. It is essential to create boundaries and be mindful of our digital habits. Consider setting designated times for technology use, turning off unnecessary notifications, and being intentional with screen time.

Mindful Technology Use

Mindful technology use involves using digital devices with awareness and intention. Instead of mindlessly scrolling through social media or engaging in constant multitasking, practice being present and attentive to your technology use. Use technology as a tool to enhance your life rather than allowing it to dominate your time and attention.

Digital Detox

A digital detox involves taking a break from digital devices for a certain period. It can be as short as a few hours or as long as a weekend or more. During a digital detox, engage in offline activities that promote relaxation, creativity, and connection with the physical world.

Benefits of Digital Detox

A digital detox allows your mind to rest and recharge. It can lead to increased mental clarity, reduced stress levels, improved sleep quality, and a greater sense of presence and focus in daily life.

Conclusion

Recognizing the effects of technology overload on our mental clarity is crucial in today's digital age. By finding balance, practicing mindful technology use, and occasionally taking digital detox breaks, you can nurture mental clarity and well-being. Remember that technology is a tool, and it is within your power to use it mindfully and intentionally to enhance your life.

Establishing Healthy Boundaries with Digital Devices

In this section, we will explore the importance of establishing healthy boundaries with digital devices to foster mental clarity and well-being in the digital age. As technology continues to play a significant role in our lives, it is essential to be mindful of how we engage with digital devices and set boundaries that support our overall well-being.

Understanding Healthy Boundaries

Healthy boundaries with digital devices involve creating limits and guidelines for their use. It means being intentional about when, where, and how we interact with technology to ensure it enhances our lives rather than becoming a source of distraction or stress.

Assessing Your Digital Habits

Take a moment to assess your current digital habits. Are you constantly checking your phone for notifications? Do you find yourself mindlessly scrolling through social media for long periods? Understanding your digital habits is the first step toward establishing healthier boundaries.

Designating Device-Free Zones and Times

Consider designating certain areas in your home or specific times of the day as device-free zones. For example, avoid using digital devices during meals, before bedtime, or first thing in the morning. Creating device-free spaces and times allows you to disconnect and be more present at the moment.

Managing Notifications

Unnecessary notifications can be a significant source of distraction. Take control of your notifications by disabling non-essential ones or setting specific times to check them. This way, you can focus on important tasks without constant interruptions.

Practicing Mindful Technology Use

Engage in mindful technology use by being present and intentional with your interactions. When you use digital devices, be aware of your thoughts and emotions, and notice how they are affected by your technology use. This awareness can help you make conscious choices about your digital habits.

Setting Personal Limits

Set personal limits on the time you spend on social media, gaming, or other digital activities. Decide how much time is reasonable for you and stick to it. Setting limits helps prevent overuse and ensures you allocate time for other essential activities and relationships.

Seeking Digital-Free Activities

Explore digital-free activities that bring you joy and fulfillment. This could include spending time in nature, pursuing hobbies, reading books, or engaging in face-to-face conversations. Balancing digital and non-digital activities enriches your life and contributes to mental clarity.

Conclusion

Establishing healthy boundaries with digital devices is vital for maintaining mental clarity and well-being in the digital age. By being mindful of your digital habits, designating device-free zones and times, managing notifications, and setting personal limits, you can create a balanced and intentional relationship with technology. Remember that you have the power to shape your digital experiences and cultivate a clear and focused mind in the digital world.

Practicing Digital Detox Techniques and Mindful Technology Use

In this section, we will delve into the practices of digital detox and mindful technology use to nurture clarity amidst the digital age. As our lives become increasingly entwined with technology, it is crucial to find moments of disconnection and cultivate a mindful approach to our digital interactions.

Understanding Digital Detox

A digital detox involves taking intentional breaks from digital devices and platforms. It is a period of disconnecting from the digital world to create space for reflection, relaxation, and reconnection with the present moment.

Benefits of Digital Detox

Digital detoxes offer numerous benefits, including reduced stress, improved focus, enhanced creativity, and better sleep quality. Stepping away from digital devices allows you to recharge and regain mental clarity.

Practical Digital Detox Techniques

1. **Device-Free Time:** Designate specific times of the day or week when you completely disconnect from digital devices. Use this time for other activities, such as reading, exercising, or spending quality time with loved ones.

2. **Screen-Free Bedroom:** Make your bedroom a screen-free zone to promote better sleep. Avoid using phones or tablets before bedtime to improve your sleep quality and wake up feeling more refreshed.

3. **Social Media Sabbatical:** Consider taking a break from social media for a few days or longer. This break allows you to recalibrate your relationship with social media and reduces comparison and information overload.

Practicing Mindful Technology Use

1. **Set Intentions:** Before using digital devices, set clear intentions for your interactions. Ask yourself why you are using the device and what you hope to achieve. This mindful approach helps you stay focused and avoid mindless scrolling.

2. **Be Present:** When using digital devices, be fully present and attentive to the task at hand. Avoid multitasking and give your full attention to one activity at a time.

3. **Mindful Check-Ins:** Throughout the day, take mindful check-ins to observe how technology use affects your emotions and well-being. If you notice feelings of stress or overwhelm, take a short break to reset.

Embracing Mindful Technology Use as a Lifestyle: Mindful technology use is not just a one-time practice but a lifestyle choice. By embracing mindfulness in your digital interactions, you can maintain mental clarity and focus on the long term.

Conclusion

Practicing digital detox and mindful technology use are powerful tools for nurturing mental clarity and well-being in the digital age. By taking intentional breaks from digital devices and cultivating mindfulness in your technology use, you can create a balanced and healthier relationship with technology. These practices empower you to reclaim your time, attention, and mental clarity amidst the digital noise.

Leveraging Technology for Enhancing Productivity and Well-being

In this section, we will explore the positive aspects of technology and how it can be harnessed to enhance your productivity and well-being. While it's essential to practice digital detox and mindful technology use, it's equally important to leverage technology as a tool for personal growth and fulfillment.

Maximizing Productivity

1. **Task Management Apps:** Use productivity apps and tools to organize your tasks, set deadlines, and track progress. These apps help you stay focused and manage your time efficiently.

2. **Note-Taking Apps:** Digital note-taking apps can streamline your thoughts and ideas, making it easier to access and organize information when needed.

3. **Time Tracking Tools:** Use time-tracking apps to monitor how you spend your time. Understanding your time usage can help you identify areas where you can improve productivity.

Enhancing Well-being

1. **Meditation and Mindfulness Apps**: Utilize meditation and mindfulness apps to cultivate inner peace and reduce stress. These apps offer guided sessions and breathing exercises to promote relaxation.

2. **Health and Fitness Apps:** Use health and fitness apps to track your physical activity, nutrition, and sleep patterns. These apps support your well-being goals and encourage healthy habits.

3. **Gratitude Journals:** Digital gratitude journals can help you cultivate a positive mindset by regularly recording moments of gratitude and appreciation.

Mindful Technology Use

While leveraging technology for productivity and well-being, remember to practice mindful technology use. Set boundaries on your tech usage, take regular breaks, and be intentional with your interactions.

Balancing Technology and Well-being

Finding a balance between technology use and well-being is key. Avoid excessive screen time and set designated periods for technology-free activities. Engage in offline hobbies, spend time in nature, and prioritize face-to-face interactions.

Conclusion

Technology can be a powerful ally in enhancing your productivity and well-being when used mindfully. By incorporating productivity tools and well-being apps into your daily life, you can optimize your time, support your health, and cultivate a more balanced and fulfilling lifestyle. Remember to maintain a mindful approach to technology use, ensuring that it enriches your life rather than detracting from it.

Chapter 7: Bringing It All Together: Sustaining Clarity in Everyday Life

Congratulations on your journey of self-discovery and growth so far! In this chapter, we will focus on integrating the valuable lessons and practices you've learned from previous chapters into your daily routines. Sustaining clarity in everyday life requires consistent effort and dedication, and by incorporating these practices, you can create a lasting positive impact on your well-being.

Integrating the Lessons and Practices from Previous Chapters into Daily Routines

Creating Daily Rituals

1. **Morning Mindfulness:** Start your day with a few moments of mindfulness. Practice deep breathing, set positive intentions, and visualize a clear and focused day ahead.

2. **Reflection Time:** Set aside time each evening for self-reflection. Review your day, celebrate achievements, and acknowledge areas where you can improve.

Incorporating Mindfulness in Activities

1. **Mindful Eating:** Practice mindful eating by savoring each bite and paying attention to the flavors and textures of your food. This can enhance your eating experience and promote better digestion.

2. **Mindful Movement:** Whether it's yoga, walking, or any form of exercise, engage in mindful movement. Be fully present in the activity and connect with your body and breath.

Consistency in Stress Management

1. **Stress Check-ins:** Regularly assess your stress levels throughout the day. If you feel overwhelmed, take short breaks to practice breathing exercises or go for a mindful walk.

2. **Prioritize Self-Care:** Make self-care a priority and set boundaries to protect your well-being. Engage in activities that nurture your mind, body, and soul.

Goal Setting and Progress Tracking

1. **Review SMART Goals:** Regularly review your SMART goals and track your progress. Celebrate small wins and adjust your goals as needed to stay aligned with your priorities.

2. **Gratitude Practice:** Continue your gratitude practice by writing down things you are thankful for each day. Gratitude can shift your focus to the positive aspects of life.

Mindful Technology Use

1. **Digital Detox Days:** Plan regular digital detox days where you disconnect from technology and focus on real-life experiences.

2. **Digital Boundaries:** Set limits on social media and screen time. Use technology with intention and be aware of how it impacts your well-being.

Conclusion

By integrating the practices from this book into your daily life, you are on a path to sustaining mental clarity, inner peace, and personal growth. Embrace the journey with an open heart, knowing that it's okay to take small steps and adjust along the way. Remember, mindfulness and clarity are ongoing practices, and every effort you make adds up to a more fulfilling and purposeful life.

Creating Supportive Habits for Maintaining Mental Clarity

In this chapter, we'll explore the significance of creating supportive habits that foster and maintain your mental clarity. These habits will serve as pillars in your journey toward a more balanced and focused life. By incorporating them into your daily routine, you'll build a strong foundation for sustaining the clarity you've cultivated so far.

Morning Rituals for Mindful Start

1. **Mindful Breathing**: Begin your day with a few minutes of deep breathing to center yourself and set a positive tone for the day ahead.

2. **Gratitude Practice:** Take a moment each morning to express gratitude for the blessings in your life. This practice can uplift your mood and enhance your overall outlook.

Organizing and Decluttering

1. **Tidy Environment:** Organize your living space to create a clutter-free environment. A tidy space promotes mental clarity and allows you to focus better.

2. **Daily Prioritization:** Start each day by identifying the most important tasks and setting clear priorities. Focus on completing these tasks before moving on to others.

Mindful Technology Use

1. **Digital Boundaries:** Set specific time limits for using social media and digital devices. Avoid checking emails and messages first thing in the morning to maintain a calm mind.

2. **Designated Tech-Free Zones:** Create tech-free zones in your home, such as the dining area or bedroom, to promote face-to-face interactions and relaxation.

Embracing Self-Care and Rest

1. **Prioritize Sleep:** Ensure you get enough restful sleep each night. A well-rested mind is more alert and better equipped to handle challenges.

2. **Recharge Activities:** Engage in activities that bring you joy and relaxation. This could be reading, spending time in nature, or pursuing a hobby.

Reflection and Gratitude

1. **Evening Reflection:** End your day with a brief reflection. Acknowledge your accomplishments, identify areas for improvement, and release any tension or stress.

2. **Gratitude Journal:** Before bedtime, write down three things you are grateful for that happened during the day. This practice can shift your focus to the positive aspects of your life.

Remember, forming new habits takes time and effort. Be patient with yourself and celebrate your progress, no matter how small. By cultivating these supportive habits, you'll create a life that fosters mental clarity, emotional well-being, and a deeper sense of fulfillment.

Nurturing Self-Care, Self-Reflection, and Self-Compassion

In this section, we'll delve into the vital practices of self-care, self-reflection, and self-compassion. These practices are essential for nurturing your well-being, gaining deeper insights into yourself, and cultivating a compassionate and understanding relationship with yourself.

The Importance of Self-Care

1. **Prioritizing Your Needs:** Make time for self-care activities that rejuvenate your body, mind, and soul. This could be taking a long bath, going for a walk, or spending quality time with loved ones.

2. **Setting Boundaries:** Learn to say no to commitments that overwhelm you and honor your need for personal space and time.

The Power of Self-Reflection

1. **Journaling:** Keep a journal to explore your thoughts, emotions, and experiences. Regular writing can provide clarity and help identify patterns in your thinking.

2. **Mindful Observation:** Practice mindful observation of your thoughts and emotions without judgment. This allows you to gain insight into your reactions and triggers.

Cultivating Self-Compassion

1. **Kindness to Yourself:** Replace self-criticism with self-compassion. Treat yourself with the same understanding and kindness you would offer to a dear friend.

2. **Embracing Imperfection:** Recognize that nobody is perfect, and it's okay to make mistakes. Embrace imperfections as part of your growth journey.

Learning from Setbacks

1. **Learning Opportunities:** View setbacks as opportunities for growth and learning. Embrace challenges as chances to build resilience and strength.

2. **Gratitude for Lessons:** Express gratitude for the lessons you've learned from difficult experiences. Every setback can be a stepping stone to greater wisdom.

Embracing Your Authentic Self

1. **Uncover Your Values:** Reflect on your core values and align your choices and actions with what truly matters to you.

2. **Authenticity in Relationships:** Surround yourself with people who appreciate and support your authentic self. Let go of relationships that drain your energy or force you to be someone you're not.

Remember, self-care, self-reflection, and self-compassion are ongoing practices that require patience and dedication. Be gentle with yourself and embrace these practices as acts of love towards yourself. By nurturing these aspects of your life, you'll deepen your connection with yourself, cultivate mental clarity, and foster a greater sense of well-being.

Embracing a Lifelong Journey of Personal Growth and Continued Decluttering

As we reach the final chapter of this book, I want to emphasize the significance of embracing a lifelong journey of personal growth and continued decluttering. The pursuit of mental clarity and well-being is not a destination but a continuous path of self-discovery and growth. By remaining committed to this journey, you can nurture your inner clarity and create a fulfilling life aligned with your values and aspirations.

Embracing Growth

1. **Openness to Change:** Embrace change as an inherent part of life. Allow yourself to evolve, adapt, and learn from new experiences.

2. **Embracing Challenges:** Embrace challenges as opportunities for growth. See them as stepping stones that lead you closer to your goals.

Continued Decluttering

1. **Decluttering the Mind:** Regularly declutter your mind by practicing mindfulness, cognitive restructuring, and positive thinking. Let go of thoughts that no longer serve you.

2. **Simplifying Your Life:** Continue simplifying various aspects of your life, including possessions, commitments, and relationships. Create space for what truly matters.

Self-Reflection and Course Correction

1. **Periodic Self-Reflection:** Set aside time for self-reflection to evaluate your progress and realign your actions with your goals and values.

2. **Flexibility and Adaptability:** Be flexible and adaptable in your journey. Understand that your goals and priorities may evolve, and that's okay.

Celebrating Progress

1. **Celebrate Achievements:** Acknowledge and celebrate the milestones you achieve on your journey. Each step forward is a testament to your growth.

2. **Practicing Gratitude:** Cultivate gratitude for the progress you've made and the lessons you've learned. Gratitude keeps you anchored in the present.

Connecting with Support

1. **Community and Support:** Seek support from like-minded individuals who are also on a path of personal growth. Share your experiences and learn from others.

2. **Mentors and Guides:** Consider seeking guidance from mentors or coaches who can provide insights and encouragement.

Remember, the journey of personal growth is unique to everyone, and there is no one-size-fits-all approach. Be patient with yourself and celebrate the process of growth. The key is to approach this journey with an open heart and an unwavering commitment to your well-being and clarity.

As you continue this path, may you discover the profound wisdom that lies within you and find fulfillment in the pursuit of clarity and personal growth.

Chapter 8: Success Stories and Testimonials

In this final chapter, we are delighted to share inspiring success stories from individuals who have embarked on their journey to declutter their minds and find clarity in their lives. These stories serve as testaments to the transformative power of the practices and techniques explored throughout this book.

Sharing Inspiring Success Stories from Individuals Who Have Decluttered Their Minds

John's Journey to Inner Peace:

John, a busy professional, shares how he felt overwhelmed by the constant noise and distractions in his life. Through mindfulness practices and self-compassion, he learned to let go of self-critical thoughts and embrace a more peaceful mindset. Today, he navigates his demanding career with a sense of calm and clarity.

Emily's Path to Purpose:

Emily struggled with a lack of direction and a feeling of stagnation in her life. By defining her values and setting meaningful goals, she found renewed purpose and motivation. She now lives with intention and fulfillment, pursuing her passions with confidence.

James' Digital Detox Transformation:

James was addicted to his digital devices, and it took a toll on his mental clarity and well-being. Through a digital detox and mindful technology use, he regained control over his digital life and reconnected with the present moment. Today, he cherishes meaningful interactions and is more present in his relationships.

Samantha's Resilience in the Face of Adversity:

Samantha faced significant life challenges that affected her mental clarity and emotional well-being. Through cognitive restructuring and positive thinking, she learned to reframe negative experiences and cultivate resilience. Now, she approaches challenges with courage and an empowered mindset.

David's Journey to Simplicity:

David was overwhelmed by clutter in his home and life. By embracing minimalism and simplifying his possessions, commitments, and daily routines, he found a newfound sense of peace and focus. Today, his decluttered space mirrors his decluttered mind.

Karen's Gratitude for the Present Moment:

Karen lived in constant worry about the future and regret about the past. Through mindfulness and gratitude practices, she learned to be fully present in the moment and appreciate life's simple joys. Now, she experiences a deeper connection with herself and her surroundings.

These success stories demonstrate that the journey to mental clarity and well-being is attainable and transformative. As you read about these experiences, may they inspire you to embark on your path of decluttering the mind and finding profound clarity in your life.

Testimonials Highlighting the Transformative Power of the Book's Strategies and Techniques

We are excited to share with you some heartfelt testimonials from individuals who have embraced the strategies and techniques presented in this book. These testimonials highlight the transformative power of decluttering the mind and cultivating mental clarity.

Testimonial 1:

"After feeling lost and overwhelmed for years, this book came into my life like a guiding light. The mindfulness practices and cognitive restructuring techniques helped me challenge my negative thought patterns and find a sense of peace within. I now approach challenges with a positive mindset,

and the mental clutter that once weighed me down has lifted. Thank you for this life-changing journey!" - Sarah

Testimonial 2:

"Digital overload was becoming a serious issue in my life, affecting my focus and relationships. This book's digital detox and mindful technology use sections were eye-opening. I now set boundaries with my devices and have rediscovered the joy of being present with loved ones. My mind feels clearer, and I am more in control of my digital habits." - Michael

Testimonial 3:

"Prioritization and goal setting were never my strong suits, leading to a lack of direction and purpose in my life. This book's guidance on defining personal values and setting SMART goals was a game-changer. I now have a clear roadmap for my future, and each day feels more purposeful and fulfilling." - Emma

Testimonial 4:

"I used to be a chronic worrier, drowning in stress and anxiety. The techniques for cultivating self-compassion and gratitude have been transformative. I now treat myself with kindness and focus on the present moment. My mind feels lighter, and I am better equipped to handle life's challenges." - Mark

Testimonial 5:

"Simplicity and minimalism were concepts I never thought would apply to my life. However, after reading this book, I decided to declutter my physical space and commitments. The result? A newfound sense of calm, clarity, and joy. Simplifying my life has made a significant impact on my mental well-being." - Lily

These testimonials exemplify the power of the practices shared in this book. We hope they inspire you to take the first steps on your journey to mental clarity and well-being. Remember, you can create profound change in your life through intentional and mindful choices.

Reinforcing the Belief that Clarity is Attainable for Every Reader

As you embark on your journey to cultivate mental clarity and declutter your mind, we want to emphasize a fundamental belief: clarity is attainable for every individual, including you.

Throughout this book, we have shared practical techniques, insightful strategies, and transformative practices that have the potential to bring about positive change in your life. Each chapter is designed to empower you to take conscious steps toward a clearer and more fulfilling existence.

It is natural to encounter challenges along the way. You may face moments of self-doubt or find certain practices more difficult to integrate into your daily routine. However, we encourage you to remember that the path to mental clarity is not linear. It is a journey of self-discovery and growth, and it is okay to take one step at a time.

Believe in yourself and your ability to bring about change. The mere fact that you have taken an interest in decluttering your mind is a testament to your determination and willingness to embrace positive transformation.

Remember that you are not alone on this journey. Countless individuals have successfully navigated the path to mental clarity using the techniques presented in this book. Their inspiring success stories stand as a testament to the power of these practices.

Be patient and compassionate with yourself. Change takes time, and cultivating mental clarity is no exception. Celebrate even the smallest victories and be kind to yourself when facing setbacks. Embrace each moment as an opportunity for growth and learning.

As you incorporate mindfulness, self-compassion, prioritization, goal-setting, and other practices into your life, trust in the process. Your mind has an incredible capacity for change and adaptation. With persistence and dedication, you can create a space of calm, focus, and serenity within.

Remember, you hold the power to create the life you desire—one filled with clarity, purpose, and well-being. Take the knowledge and tools from this book, apply them in your daily life, and watch as mental clutter gradually makes way for profound clarity.

We believe in you, and we are cheering you on every step of the way.

Chapter 9: Conclusion

Summarizing key takeaways and lessons learned

As we conclude this book, it is essential to reflect on the key takeaways and lessons that we have explored throughout our journey toward cultivating mental clarity. The path to decluttering the mind and finding inner peace is not always easy, but it is undoubtedly rewarding. Let's recap some of the vital insights we have gained:

- **Mindfulness and Self-Awareness:** We have learned the profound significance of mindfulness and self-awareness in our pursuit of mental clarity. By turning inward and developing a deeper understanding of our thoughts, emotions, and behaviors, we can recognize patterns, triggers, and limiting beliefs that contribute to mental clutter.

- **Simplification and Minimalism:** Simplifying our physical environment and various aspects of life can have a profound impact on mental clarity. Letting go of excess possessions, commitments, and distractions allows us to create space for clarity to emerge.

- **Stress Management and Relaxation:** Identifying sources of stress and learning stress reduction techniques are essential for fostering mental well-being. Breathing exercises, mindfulness-based stress reduction, and self-care activities help us navigate challenges with resilience and serenity.

- **Cognitive Restructuring and Positive Thinking:** Reshaping our thoughts and cultivating a positive mindset enable us to break free from self-limiting beliefs and embrace empowering perspectives. By reframing negative experiences and fostering self-compassion and gratitude, we declutter our minds and enhance mental well-being.

- **Prioritization and Goal Setting:** Defining personal values and aligning them with SMART goals give us direction and purpose. By establishing healthy boundaries and staying motivated, we can achieve a sense of fulfillment, accomplishment, and clarity.

- **Digital Detox and Mindful Technology Use:** Recognizing the effects of technology overload and practicing digital detox techniques help us find balance amidst the digital age. Mindful technology use ensures that we leverage technology to enhance productivity and well-being while avoiding unnecessary distractions.

- **Sustaining Clarity in Everyday Life:** By integrating the lessons and practices from previous chapters into our daily routines, creating supportive habits, and nurturing self-care and self-compassion, we can sustain mental clarity and well-being in our day-to-day lives.

- **Success Stories and Testimonials**: We have been inspired by the success stories of individuals who have decluttered their minds and witnessed the transformative power of the book's strategies and techniques.

Throughout this book, we have emphasized that mental clarity is attainable for every reader. It is a lifelong journey of personal growth and continued decluttering. Remember that progress may not always be linear, and setbacks are a natural part of the process. Embrace self-compassion and patience as you navigate this transformative journey.

By cultivating self-awareness, simplifying your life, managing stress, and embracing positive thinking, you can create a profound shift in your mental clarity and overall well-being. The key is to stay committed, take small steps consistently, and be open to learning and growth.

We hope that the knowledge and tools you have acquired in this book serve as a reliable guide on your path to mental clarity and inner peace.

Remember, the power to declutter your mind and foster a sense of clarity and purpose lies within you.

Encouraging readers to embrace their newfound clarity and continue their growth journey

Congratulations on completing this journey toward cultivating mental clarity and inner peace. As you reflect on the insights and practices you have gained throughout this book, we encourage you to embrace your newfound clarity and continue your growth journey.

Remember that mental clarity is not a destination but an ongoing process. It is okay to experience moments of challenge and uncertainty along the way. Be gentle with yourself and celebrate the progress you have made. Each step you take towards self-awareness, simplification, and positive thinking contributes to your overall well-being and fulfillment.

As you navigate your daily life, be mindful of the choices you make. Prioritize activities and commitments that align with your values and goals. Set SMART goals and stay committed to achieving them. Embrace the power of resilience and self-compassion, for they will support you in overcoming obstacles and staying motivated on your path.

In this digital age, practice mindful technology use and remember the importance of regular digital detox. Create boundaries that protect your time and energy, allowing you to focus on what truly matters.

Above all, continue to nurture self-care and self-reflection. Dedicate time to activities that bring you joy and recharge your spirit. Cultivate a positive mindset, and when negative thoughts arise, remember that you have the power to reframe them and choose empowering perspectives.

In times of uncertainty and challenge, draw from the lessons you have learned in stress management and relaxation. Breathe deeply, practice mindfulness, and be kind to yourself. Trust in your inner strength and resilience.

Lastly, seek inspiration from the success stories and testimonials shared in this book. Know that you are not alone on this journey. Many have walked a similar path and found clarity, peace, and fulfillment. You, too, can create a life of purpose and joy.

Embrace this lifelong journey of personal growth and continued decluttering. Keep an open heart and mind, always willing to learn and grow. As you do so, you will discover the immense potential within you, and your clarity will radiate in every aspect of your life.

We are honored to have been part of your journey, and we wish you all the best in your pursuit of mental clarity and well-being.

Offering additional resources and recommendations for further exploration

As you continue your journey toward cultivating mental clarity and embracing a more fulfilling life, we encourage you to explore further resources and recommendations that can support your growth and development. Here are some additional resources to consider:

- **Books on Mindfulness and Meditation:** Dive deeper into the practices of mindfulness and meditation with books written by renowned authors such as Jon Kabat-Zinn, Eckhart Tolle, and Thich Nhat Hanh. These authors offer valuable insights and techniques for developing present-moment awareness and inner peace.

- **Mindfulness Apps:** Explore various mindfulness apps available on your smartphone or tablet. Apps like Headspace, Calm, and Insight Timer provide guided meditations, breathing exercises, and relaxation techniques to help you incorporate mindfulness into your daily life.

- **Personal Development Workshops:** Consider attending workshops or seminars focused on personal development and well-being. These events offer a supportive environment to explore new tools and strategies for achieving clarity and self-growth.

- **Online Courses on Stress Management:** Look for online courses that specialize in stress management and relaxation techniques. Platforms like Coursera, Udemy, and Mindfulness X offer courses led by experts in the field.

- **Podcasts on Mental Well-being:** Podcasts are an excellent way to stay motivated and inspired. Seek out podcasts that discuss topics related to mindfulness, self-compassion, and decluttering the mind.

- **Nature and Outdoor Activities:** Spending time in nature can be incredibly rejuvenating and beneficial for mental clarity. Consider incorporating outdoor activities like hiking, gardening, or simply taking a walk in the park into your routine.

- **Journaling:** Start a journaling practice to explore your thoughts and emotions. Writing can be a powerful tool for self-discovery and introspection.

- **Mindful Eating and Nutrition:** Consider exploring the relationship between nutrition and mental well-being. Learn about mindful eating practices and how they can contribute to your overall clarity and health.

Remember, the journey of personal growth is unique to everyone. Be open to exploring various resources and find what resonates best with you. Embrace the process with patience and self-compassion, knowing that each step you take brings you closer to the clarity and fulfillment you seek.

We hope these additional resources enrich your journey and support you in embracing a life filled with clarity, purpose, and joy.